Mommy, I Thought You Said Black Was Beautiful

By Phillip White
and
Jeresha White

Mommy, I Thought You Said Black Was Beautiful

co-author Jeresha White

Illustrated by Stacy Hummel

Published by November Media Publishing

To my children, your children, our children.
I see you, I hear you. You are loved, needed, wanted, and appreciated.

The world is yours, bless it with your innocence.

Mommy, why do I always see
people that look like me die on T.V.?
You say "Black is beautiful," and "Be all you can be!"
but I could end up white chalk in the street.

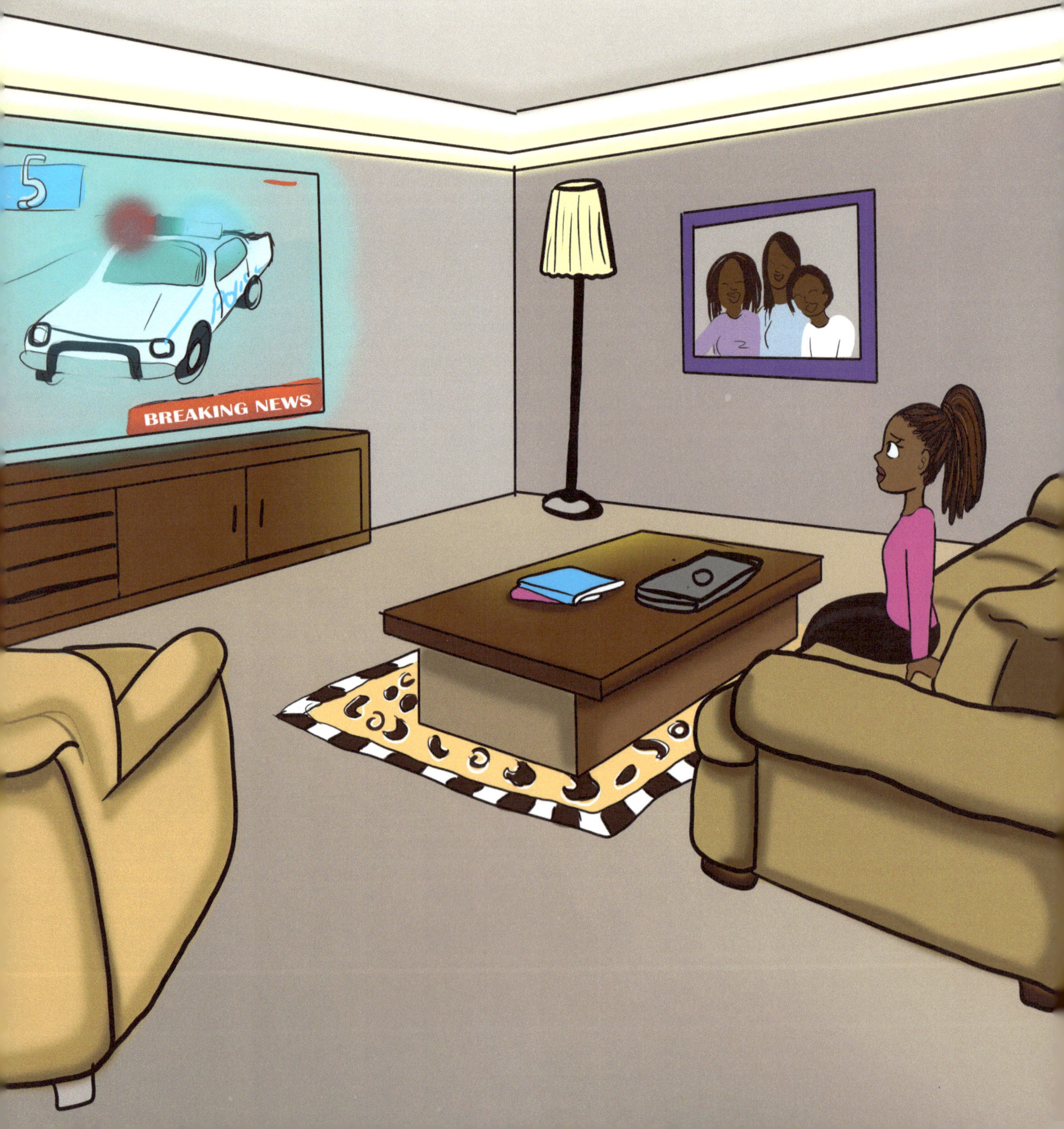

Daughter, what did you see when you watched T.V.?
What has you upset with so many questions for me?

Dad, I saw Black people who look like me, hurting on T.V. and yelling "I Can't Breathe!"

I saw protests turn violent,
the cries turned into roars,
people who are tired and can't take it no more,
broken glass and fire, with riots and war.
They even burned down the Candy Lady's store!

In school we learn about Martin Luther King,
but peace and freedom are things I don't see.

Is it how I dress Mommy?
Is it how I speak?
Is it my eyes, ears, nose, or my cheeks?

Is it my hair or the sneakers on my feet?
Why are they hurting people who look just like me?

I had a scary dream last night that woke me out of my sleep.
Everyone was at a funeral, and the funeral was for me.
Dad, I don't think Black is a safe color to be!
Dad, I thought you said Black was beautiful, but that is not what I see!

My child I am proud of your discussion with me,
But remember Black is a beautiful color to be.
I know on T.V. you see nothing but grief,
but use that to fight harder because nothing is free.

Speak loud and stand up for hundreds to see.

Words with life can make roses grow from concrete.

Dad, sometimes being peaceful seems useless to me.
I am afraid one day, they'll do something to me!
All those names they say on the T.V.,
were people laughing, playing, and running like me.
What if the next hashtag is created for me?

Dad, what if one day the Police come for me
I'll raise my hands and comply; it still may not
go well for me.
If they miss, I was lucky.
If they don't then I die,
another city filled with anger
As our Black people cry.

Rosa Parks fought for me to sit in the front seat,
but none of the other kids like to even sit next to me!

Sometimes being Black is not a fun color to be,
None of the kids use Black crayons when they color with me.

Mommy, Police put dads in prison the same color as me.
Mommy, They hurt sisters and brothers the same color as me
Mommy, everyone who is poor are the same color as me.
There's got to be more for people the same color as me! —

I think that red, green, yellow are good colors to be
Because they never get hurt like people the same color as me.

Mommy, open sores never heal.
You can't heal open sores,
Because as soon as one heals, they open one more.
So what will it take for the sick to get better?
Must I die for my color to bring us together?

Daughter, you have got to see,
Black is a very beautiful color to be.
In fact, it's a color that is very unique.
This is a time for you to stand up for the world to see!
Just stand strong, you can make a difference,
you can be all that you want to be!
Because there is power in every Black
boy and Black girl,
That I want you to see.

My child, the harder the struggle, the greater the win.
Thank God for the color he made your skin.
You've done nothing wrong, so never be ashamed!
You're a beautiful black picture in a solid gold frame.

But, no dad, that doesn't seem true.
The truth is sadder,
It makes me madder
To realize that all colors really don't matter.

If all lives mattered, they forgot the Black ones
the Black mothers and fathers, the daughters and sons,
I shouldn't be murdered because of my skin.
Is my color a curse, a crime, or a sin?

My child, you can overcome all the pain that you see.
You can't let it stop you from being all you can be.
Aim for the stars and look how far we came.
All the crayons in the box were created the same!

Daughter, you've got to trust and believe
the Black color you are, was made wonderfully!
You and all of the children the same color as you
are made to matter like the other colors too,
daughter, because black is beautiful, and so are you.

www.ingramcontent.com/pod-product-compliance
Lightning Source LLC
LaVergne TN
LVHW071520210825
819133LV00003B/9
* 9 7 8 1 7 3 5 4 5 4 2 2 1 *